DR. LIMA'S PLANNER FOR NEURODIVERSE PEOPLE

THIS PLANNER BELONGS TO:

_____

"When I dare to be powerful — to use my strength in the service of my vision — then it becomes less and less important whether I am afraid."

— AUDRE LORDE

SUN	MON	TUES	WED
☐	☐	☐	☐
☐	☐	☐	☐
☐	☐	☐	☐
☐	☐	☐	☐
☐	☐	☐	☐

GOALS

_____   _____

_____   _____

_____   _____

_____   _____

THURS	FRI	SAT	_____
☐	☐	☐	**NOTES**
☐	☐	☐	
☐	☐	☐	
☐	☐	☐	
☐	☐	☐	

PRIORITIES

SMALL VICTORIES

THOUGHTS AND DOODLES

APPOINTMENTS

PERSON:
DATE:
LOCATION:

PERSON:
DATE:
LOCATION:

PERSON:
DATE:
LOCATION:

PERSON:
DATE:
LOCATION:

PERSON:
DATE:
LOCATION:

PERSON:
DATE:
LOCATION:

PERSON:
DATE:
LOCATION:

I GOT IT DONE

- ⬡
- ⬡
- ⬡
- ⬡
- ⬡
- ⬡
- ⬡
- ⬡
- ⬡
- ⬡
- ⬡
- ⬡
- ⬡
- ⬡
- ⬡
- ⬡
- ⬡
- ⬡
- ⬡
- ⬡
- ⬡
- ⬡
- ⬡
- ⬡
- ⬡
- ⬡
- ⬡
- ⬡

THIS MONTH

IMPORTANT DATES

THINGS I CAN DO FOR MYSELF THAT WOULD BRING JOY OR HELP ME RECHARGE

PERSON (S) I NEED TO CONNECT WITH

DECISION MAKING

PROJECT: _____

IS IT URGENT?

	YES	NO
IS IT IMPORTANT? YES	STEPS TO DO IT NOW:	PLAN OF ACTION:
NO	DELEGATE TO:	DISCART IT

SELF-CARE CHECKLIST

ACTION	M	T	W	T	F	S	S
	☐	☐	☐	☐	☐	☐	☐
	☐	☐	☐	☐	☐	☐	☐
	☐	☐	☐	☐	☐	☐	☐
	☐	☐	☐	☐	☐	☐	☐
	☐	☐	☐	☐	☐	☐	☐
	☐	☐	☐	☐	☐	☐	☐
	☐	☐	☐	☐	☐	☐	☐
	☐	☐	☐	☐	☐	☐	☐
	☐	☐	☐	☐	☐	☐	☐
	☐	☐	☐	☐	☐	☐	☐

PRODUCTIVITY TRACKER

START	END	TASK	START	END	TASK

PRODUCTIVITY TRACKER

START	END	TASK	START	END	TASK

	SUN	MON	TUES	WED
☐				
	☐	☐	☐	☐
	☐	☐	☐	☐
	☐	☐	☐	☐
	☐	☐	☐	☐
	☐	☐	☐	☐

GOALS

_____

_____

_____

_____

| THURS | FRI | SAT | _____ |

NOTES

PRIORITIES

SMALL VICTORIES

NOTES

THOUGHTS AND DOODLES

APPOINTMENTS

PERSON:
DATE:
LOCATION:

PERSON:
DATE:
LOCATION:

PERSON:
DATE:
LOCATION:

PERSON:
DATE:
LOCATION:

PERSON:
DATE:
LOCATION:

PERSON:
DATE:
LOCATION:

PERSON:
DATE:
LOCATION:

I GOT IT DONE

- ⬡
- ⬡
- ⬡
- ⬡
- ⬡
- ⬡
- ⬡
- ⬡
- ⬡
- ⬡
- ⬡
- ⬡
- ⬡
- ⬡
- ⬡
- ⬡
- ⬡
- ⬡
- ⬡
- ⬡
- ⬡
- ⬡
- ⬡
- ⬡
- ⬡
- ⬡

THIS MONTH

IMPORTANT DATES

THINGS I CAN DO FOR MYSELF THAT WOULD BRING JOY OR HELP ME RECHARGE

PERSON(S) I NEED TO CONNECT WITH

DECISION MAKING

PROJECT: _____

IS IT URGENT?

	YES	NO
IS IT IMPORTANT? YES	STEPS TO DO IT NOW:	PLAN OF ACTION:
NO	DELEGATE TO:	DISCART IT

SELF-CARE CHECKLIST

ACTION	M	T	W	T	F	S	S
	☐	☐	☐	☐	☐	☐	☐
	☐	☐	☐	☐	☐	☐	☐
	☐	☐	☐	☐	☐	☐	☐
	☐	☐	☐	☐	☐	☐	☐
	☐	☐	☐	☐	☐	☐	☐
	☐	☐	☐	☐	☐	☐	☐
	☐	☐	☐	☐	☐	☐	☐
	☐	☐	☐	☐	☐	☐	☐
	☐	☐	☐	☐	☐	☐	☐
	☐	☐	☐	☐	☐	☐	☐

PRODUCTIVITY TRACKER

START	END	TASK	START	END	TASK

PRODUCTIVITY TRACKER

START	END	TASK	START	END	TASK

SUN	MON	TUES	WED
☐	☐	☐	☐
☐	☐	☐	☐
☐	☐	☐	☐
☐	☐	☐	☐
☐	☐	☐	☐

GOALS

_____

_____

_____

_____

THURS **FRI** **SAT** _____

NOTES

PRIORITIES **SMALL VICTORIES**

NOTES

THOUGHTS AND DOODLES

APPOINTMENTS

PERSON:

DATE:

LOCATION:

PERSON:

DATE:

LOCATION:

PERSON:

DATE:

LOCATION:

PERSON:

DATE:

LOCATION:

PERSON:

DATE:

LOCATION:

PERSON:

DATE:

LOCATION:

PERSON:

DATE:

LOCATION:

I GOT IT DONE

- ⬡
- ⬡
- ⬡
- ⬡
- ⬡
- ⬡
- ⬡
- ⬡
- ⬡
- ⬡
- ⬡
- ⬡
- ⬡
- ⬡
- ⬡
- ⬡
- ⬡
- ⬡
- ⬡
- ⬡
- ⬡
- ⬡
- ⬡
- ⬡
- ⬡
- ⬡
- ⬡

THIS MONTH

IMPORTANT DATES

THINGS I CAN DO FOR MYSELF THAT WOULD BRING JOY OR HELP ME RECHARGE

PERSON (S) I NEED TO CONNECT WITH

DECISION MAKING

PROJECT: _____

IS IT URGENT?

	YES	NO
IS IT IMPORTANT? YES	STEPS TO DO IT NOW:	PLAN OF ACTION:
NO	DELEGATE TO:	DISCART IT

SELF-CARE CHECKLIST

ACTION	M	T	W	T	F	S	S
	☐	☐	☐	☐	☐	☐	☐
	☐	☐	☐	☐	☐	☐	☐
	☐	☐	☐	☐	☐	☐	☐
	☐	☐	☐	☐	☐	☐	☐
	☐	☐	☐	☐	☐	☐	☐
	☐	☐	☐	☐	☐	☐	☐
	☐	☐	☐	☐	☐	☐	☐
	☐	☐	☐	☐	☐	☐	☐
	☐	☐	☐	☐	☐	☐	☐
	☐	☐	☐	☐	☐	☐	☐

PRODUCTIVITY TRACKER

START	END	TASK	START	END	TASK

PRODUCTIVITY TRACKER

START	END	TASK	START	END	TASK

SUN	MON	TUES	WED
☐	☐	☐	☐
☐	☐	☐	☐
☐	☐	☐	☐
☐	☐	☐	☐
☐	☐	☐	☐

GOALS

_____

_____

_____

_____

| THURS | FRI | SAT | _____ |

NOTES

PRIORITIES   **SMALL VICTORIES**

NOTES

THOUGHTS AND DOODLES

APPOINTMENTS

PERSON:
DATE:
LOCATION:

PERSON:
DATE:
LOCATION:

PERSON:
DATE:
LOCATION:

PERSON:
DATE:
LOCATION:

PERSON:
DATE:
LOCATION:

PERSON:
DATE:
LOCATION:

PERSON:
DATE:
LOCATION:

I GOT IT DONE

- ⬡
- ⬡
- ⬡
- ⬡
- ⬡
- ⬡
- ⬡
- ⬡
- ⬡
- ⬡
- ⬡
- ⬡
- ⬡
- ⬡
- ⬡
- ⬡
- ⬡
- ⬡
- ⬡
- ⬡
- ⬡
- ⬡
- ⬡
- ⬡
- ⬡
- ⬡
- ⬡
- ⬡

THIS MONTH

IMPORTANT DATES

THINGS I CAN DO FOR MYSELF THAT WOULD BRING JOY OR HELP ME RECHARGE

PERSON (S) I NEED TO CONNECT WITH

DECISION MAKING

PROJECT: _____

IS IT URGENT?

	YES	NO
IS IT IMPORTANT? YES	STEPS TO DO IT NOW:	PLAN OF ACTION:
NO	DELEGATE TO:	DISCARD IT

SELF-CARE CHECKLIST

ACTION	M	T	W	T	F	S	S
	☐	☐	☐	☐	☐	☐	☐
	☐	☐	☐	☐	☐	☐	☐
	☐	☐	☐	☐	☐	☐	☐
	☐	☐	☐	☐	☐	☐	☐
	☐	☐	☐	☐	☐	☐	☐
	☐	☐	☐	☐	☐	☐	☐
	☐	☐	☐	☐	☐	☐	☐
	☐	☐	☐	☐	☐	☐	☐
	☐	☐	☐	☐	☐	☐	☐
	☐	☐	☐	☐	☐	☐	☐

PRODUCTIVITY TRACKER

START	END	TASK	START	END	TASK

PRODUCTIVITY TRACKER

START	END	TASK	START	END	TASK

SUN	MON	TUES	WED
☐	☐	☐	☐
☐	☐	☐	☐
☐	☐	☐	☐
☐	☐	☐	☐
☐	☐	☐	☐

GOALS

_____
_____
_____
_____

THURS	FRI	SAT	_____
☐	☐	☐	**NOTES**
☐	☐	☐	
☐	☐	☐	
☐	☐	☐	
☐	☐	☐	

PRIORITIES

SMALL VICTORIES

NOTES

THOUGHTS AND DOODLES

APPOINTMENTS

PERSON:
DATE:
LOCATION:

PERSON:
DATE:
LOCATION:

PERSON:
DATE:
LOCATION:

PERSON:
DATE:
LOCATION:

PERSON:
DATE:
LOCATION:

PERSON:
DATE:
LOCATION:

PERSON:
DATE:
LOCATION:

I GOT IT DONE

◯
◯
◯
◯
◯
◯
◯
◯
◯
◯
◯
◯
◯
◯
◯
◯
◯
◯
◯
◯
◯
◯
◯
◯
◯
◯
◯
◯
◯
◯

THIS MONTH

IMPORTANT DATES

THINGS I CAN DO FOR MYSELF THAT WOULD BRING JOY OR HELP ME RECHARGE

PERSON (S) I NEED TO CONNECT WITH

DECISION MAKING

PROJECT: _____

IS IT URGENT?

	YES	NO
IS IT IMPORTANT? YES	STEPS TO DO IT NOW:	PLAN OF ACTION:
NO	DELEGATE TO:	DISCART IT

SELF-CARE CHECKLIST

ACTION	M	T	W	T	F	S	S
	☐	☐	☐	☐	☐	☐	☐
	☐	☐	☐	☐	☐	☐	☐
	☐	☐	☐	☐	☐	☐	☐
	☐	☐	☐	☐	☐	☐	☐
	☐	☐	☐	☐	☐	☐	☐
	☐	☐	☐	☐	☐	☐	☐
	☐	☐	☐	☐	☐	☐	☐
	☐	☐	☐	☐	☐	☐	☐
	☐	☐	☐	☐	☐	☐	☐
	☐	☐	☐	☐	☐	☐	☐

PRODUCTIVITY TRACKER

START	END	TASK	START	END	TASK

PRODUCTIVITY TRACKER

START	END	TASK	START	END	TASK

SUN	MON	TUES	WED
☐	☐	☐	☐
☐	☐	☐	☐
☐	☐	☐	☐
☐	☐	☐	☐
☐	☐	☐	☐

GOALS

_____

_____

_____

_____

| THURS | FRI | SAT | _____ |

NOTES

PRIORITIES

SMALL VICTORIES

NOTES

THOUGHTS AND DOODLES

APPOINTMENTS

PERSON:
DATE:
LOCATION:

PERSON:
DATE:
LOCATION:

PERSON:
DATE:
LOCATION:

PERSON:
DATE:
LOCATION:

PERSON:
DATE:
LOCATION:

PERSON:
DATE:
LOCATION:

PERSON:
DATE:
LOCATION:

I GOT IT DONE

- ⬡
- ⬡
- ⬡
- ⬡
- ⬡
- ⬡
- ⬡
- ⬡
- ⬡
- ⬡
- ⬡
- ⬡
- ⬡
- ⬡
- ⬡
- ⬡
- ⬡
- ⬡
- ⬡
- ⬡
- ⬡
- ⬡
- ⬡
- ⬡
- ⬡
- ⬡
- ⬡
- ⬡

THIS MONTH

IMPORTANT DATES

THINGS I CAN DO FOR MYSELF THAT WOULD BRING JOY OR HELP ME RECHARGE

PERSON (S) I NEED TO CONNECT WITH

DECISION MAKING

PROJECT: _____

IS IT URGENT?

	YES	NO
IS IT IMPORTANT? YES	STEPS TO DO IT NOW:	PLAN OF ACTION:
NO	DELEGATE TO:	DISCART IT

SELF-CARE CHECKLIST

ACTION	M	T	W	T	F	S	S
	☐	☐	☐	☐	☐	☐	☐
	☐	☐	☐	☐	☐	☐	☐
	☐	☐	☐	☐	☐	☐	☐
	☐	☐	☐	☐	☐	☐	☐
	☐	☐	☐	☐	☐	☐	☐
	☐	☐	☐	☐	☐	☐	☐
	☐	☐	☐	☐	☐	☐	☐
	☐	☐	☐	☐	☐	☐	☐
	☐	☐	☐	☐	☐	☐	☐
	☐	☐	☐	☐	☐	☐	☐
	☐	☐	☐	☐	☐	☐	☐

PRODUCTIVITY TRACKER

START	END	TASK	START	END	TASK

PRODUCTIVITY TRACKER

START	END	TASK	START	END	TASK

SUN	MON	TUES	WED
☐	☐	☐	☐
☐	☐	☐	☐
☐	☐	☐	☐
☐	☐	☐	☐
☐	☐	☐	☐

GOALS

_____

_____

_____

_____

THURS   **FRI**   **SAT**   _____

NOTES

PRIORITIES   **SMALL VICTORIES**

NOTES

THOUGHTS AND DOODLES

APPOINTMENTS

PERSON:
DATE:
LOCATION:

PERSON:
DATE:
LOCATION:

PERSON:
DATE:
LOCATION:

PERSON:
DATE:
LOCATION:

PERSON:
DATE:
LOCATION:

PERSON:
DATE:
LOCATION:

PERSON:
DATE:
LOCATION:

I GOT IT DONE

○
○
○
○
○
○
○
○
○
○
○
○
○
○
○
○
○
○
○
○
○
○
○
○
○
○
○
○
○

THIS MONTH

IMPORTANT DATES

THINGS I CAN DO FOR MYSELF THAT WOULD BRING JOY OR HELP ME RECHARGE

PERSON(S) I NEED TO CONNECT WITH

DECISION MAKING

PROJECT: _____

IS IT URGENT?

	YES	NO
IS IT IMPORTANT? YES	STEPS TO DO IT NOW:	PLAN OF ACTION:
NO	DELEGATE TO:	DISCART IT

SELF-CARE CHECKLIST

ACTION	M	T	W	T	F	S	S
	☐	☐	☐	☐	☐	☐	☐
	☐	☐	☐	☐	☐	☐	☐
	☐	☐	☐	☐	☐	☐	☐
	☐	☐	☐	☐	☐	☐	☐
	☐	☐	☐	☐	☐	☐	☐
	☐	☐	☐	☐	☐	☐	☐
	☐	☐	☐	☐	☐	☐	☐
	☐	☐	☐	☐	☐	☐	☐
	☐	☐	☐	☐	☐	☐	☐
	☐	☐	☐	☐	☐	☐	☐

PRODUCTIVITY TRACKER

START	END	TASK	START	END	TASK

PRODUCTIVITY TRACKER

START	END	TASK	START	END	TASK

	SUN	MON	TUES	WED
☐				
☐				
☐				
☐				
☐				

GOALS

_____

_____

_____

| THURS | FRI | SAT | _____ |

NOTES

PRIORITIES

SMALL VICTORIES

NOTES

THOUGHTS AND DOODLES

APPOINTMENTS

PERSON:
DATE:
LOCATION:

PERSON:
DATE:
LOCATION:

PERSON:
DATE:
LOCATION:

PERSON:
DATE:
LOCATION:

PERSON:
DATE:
LOCATION:

PERSON:
DATE:
LOCATION:

PERSON:
DATE:
LOCATION:

I GOT IT DONE

- ⬡
- ⬡
- ⬡
- ⬡
- ⬡
- ⬡
- ⬡
- ⬡
- ⬡
- ⬡
- ⬡
- ⬡
- ⬡
- ⬡
- ⬡
- ⬡
- ⬡
- ⬡
- ⬡
- ⬡
- ⬡
- ⬡
- ⬡
- ⬡
- ⬡
- ⬡
- ⬡
- ⬡

THIS MONTH

IMPORTANT DATES

THINGS I CAN DO FOR MYSELF THAT WOULD BRING JOY OR HELP ME RECHARGE

PERSON(S) I NEED TO CONNECT WITH

DECISION MAKING

PROJECT: _____

IS IT URGENT?

	YES	NO
IS IT IMPORTANT? YES	STEPS TO DO IT NOW:	PLAN OF ACTION:
NO	DELEGATE TO:	DISCART IT

SELF-CARE CHECKLIST

ACTION	M	T	W	T	F	S	S
	☐	☐	☐	☐	☐	☐	☐
	☐	☐	☐	☐	☐	☐	☐
	☐	☐	☐	☐	☐	☐	☐
	☐	☐	☐	☐	☐	☐	☐
	☐	☐	☐	☐	☐	☐	☐
	☐	☐	☐	☐	☐	☐	☐
	☐	☐	☐	☐	☐	☐	☐
	☐	☐	☐	☐	☐	☐	☐
	☐	☐	☐	☐	☐	☐	☐
	☐	☐	☐	☐	☐	☐	☐

PRODUCTIVITY TRACKER

START	END	TASK	START	END	TASK

PRODUCTIVITY TRACKER

START	END	TASK	START	END	TASK

SUN	MON	TUES	WED
☐	☐	☐	☐
☐	☐	☐	☐
☐	☐	☐	☐
☐	☐	☐	☐
☐	☐	☐	☐

GOALS

_____   _____
_____   _____
_____   _____
_____   _____

| THURS | FRI | SAT | _____ |

NOTES

PRIORITIES   **SMALL VICTORIES**

NOTES

THOUGHTS AND DOODLES

APPOINTMENTS

PERSON:
DATE:
LOCATION:

PERSON:
DATE:
LOCATION:

PERSON:
DATE:
LOCATION:

PERSON:
DATE:
LOCATION:

PERSON:
DATE:
LOCATION:

PERSON:
DATE:
LOCATION:

PERSON:
DATE:
LOCATION:

I GOT IT DONE

◯ ◯

THIS MONTH

IMPORTANT DATES

THINGS I CAN DO FOR MYSELF THAT WOULD BRING JOY OR HELP ME RECHARGE

PERSON(S) I NEED TO CONNECT WITH

DECISION MAKING

PROJECT: _____

IS IT URGENT?

	YES	NO
IS IT IMPORTANT? YES	STEPS TO DO IT NOW:	PLAN OF ACTION:
NO	DELEGATE TO:	DISCART IT

SELF-CARE CHECKLIST

ACTION	M	T	W	T	F	S	S
	☐	☐	☐	☐	☐	☐	☐
	☐	☐	☐	☐	☐	☐	☐
	☐	☐	☐	☐	☐	☐	☐
	☐	☐	☐	☐	☐	☐	☐
	☐	☐	☐	☐	☐	☐	☐
	☐	☐	☐	☐	☐	☐	☐
	☐	☐	☐	☐	☐	☐	☐
	☐	☐	☐	☐	☐	☐	☐
	☐	☐	☐	☐	☐	☐	☐
	☐	☐	☐	☐	☐	☐	☐

PRODUCTIVITY TRACKER

START	END	TASK	START	END	TASK

PRODUCTIVITY TRACKER

START	END	TASK	START	END	TASK

	SUN	MON	TUES	WED
☐	☐	☐	☐	☐
☐	☐	☐	☐	☐
☐	☐	☐	☐	☐
☐	☐	☐	☐	☐
☐	☐	☐	☐	☐

GOALS

_____

_____

_____

_____

| THURS | FRI | SAT | _____ |

NOTES

PRIORITIES

SMALL VICTORIES

NOTES

THOUGHTS AND DOODLES

APPOINTMENTS

PERSON:
DATE:
LOCATION:

PERSON:
DATE:
LOCATION:

PERSON:
DATE:
LOCATION:

PERSON:
DATE:
LOCATION:

PERSON:
DATE:
LOCATION:

PERSON:
DATE:
LOCATION:

PERSON:
DATE:
LOCATION:

I GOT IT DONE

- ⬡
- ⬡
- ⬡
- ⬡
- ⬡
- ⬡
- ⬡
- ⬡
- ⬡
- ⬡
- ⬡
- ⬡
- ⬡
- ⬡
- ⬡
- ⬡
- ⬡
- ⬡
- ⬡
- ⬡
- ⬡
- ⬡
- ⬡
- ⬡
- ⬡
- ⬡
- ⬡
- ⬡
- ⬡

THIS MONTH

IMPORTANT DATES

THINGS I CAN DO FOR MYSELF THAT WOULD BRING JOY OR HELP ME RECHARGE

PERSON(S) I NEED TO CONNECT WITH

DECISION MAKING

PROJECT: _____

IS IT URGENT?

	YES	NO
IS IT IMPORTANT? YES	STEPS TO DO IT NOW:	PLAN OF ACTION:
NO	DELEGATE TO:	DISCART IT

SELF-CARE CHECKLIST

ACTION	M	T	W	T	F	S	S
	☐	☐	☐	☐	☐	☐	☐
	☐	☐	☐	☐	☐	☐	☐
	☐	☐	☐	☐	☐	☐	☐
	☐	☐	☐	☐	☐	☐	☐
	☐	☐	☐	☐	☐	☐	☐
	☐	☐	☐	☐	☐	☐	☐
	☐	☐	☐	☐	☐	☐	☐
	☐	☐	☐	☐	☐	☐	☐
	☐	☐	☐	☐	☐	☐	☐
	☐	☐	☐	☐	☐	☐	☐

PRODUCTIVITY TRACKER

START	END	TASK	START	END	TASK

PRODUCTIVITY TRACKER

START	END	TASK	START	END	TASK

SUN	MON	TUES	WED
☐	☐	☐	☐
☐	☐	☐	☐
☐	☐	☐	☐
☐	☐	☐	☐
☐	☐	☐	☐

GOALS

_____   _____

_____   _____

_____   _____

_____   _____

THURS	FRI	SAT	_____
☐	☐	☐	**NOTES**
☐	☐	☐	
☐	☐	☐	
☐	☐	☐	
☐	☐	☐	

PRIORITIES

SMALL VICTORIES

NOTES

THOUGHTS AND DOODLES

APPOINTMENTS

PERSON:
DATE:
LOCATION:

PERSON:
DATE:
LOCATION:

PERSON:
DATE:
LOCATION:

PERSON:
DATE:
LOCATION:

PERSON:
DATE:
LOCATION:

PERSON:
DATE:
LOCATION:

PERSON:
DATE:
LOCATION:

I GOT IT DONE

THIS MONTH

IMPORTANT DATES

THINGS I CAN DO FOR MYSELF THAT WOULD BRING JOY OR HELP ME RECHARGE

PERSON (S) I NEED TO CONNECT WITH

DECISION MAKING

PROJECT: _____

IS IT URGENT?

	YES	NO
IS IT IMPORTANT? YES	STEPS TO DO IT NOW:	PLAN OF ACTION:
NO	DELEGATE TO:	DISCART IT

SELF-CARE CHECKLIST

ACTION	M	T	W	T	F	S	S
	☐	☐	☐	☐	☐	☐	☐
	☐	☐	☐	☐	☐	☐	☐
	☐	☐	☐	☐	☐	☐	☐
	☐	☐	☐	☐	☐	☐	☐
	☐	☐	☐	☐	☐	☐	☐
	☐	☐	☐	☐	☐	☐	☐
	☐	☐	☐	☐	☐	☐	☐
	☐	☐	☐	☐	☐	☐	☐
	☐	☐	☐	☐	☐	☐	☐
	☐	☐	☐	☐	☐	☐	☐

PRODUCTIVITY TRACKER

START	END	TASK	START	END	TASK

PRODUCTIVITY TRACKER

START	END	TASK	START	END	TASK

SUN	MON	TUES	WED
☐	☐	☐	☐
☐	☐	☐	☐
☐	☐	☐	☐
☐	☐	☐	☐
☐	☐	☐	☐

GOALS

_____   _____
_____   _____
_____   _____
_____   _____

| THURS | FRI | SAT | _____ |

NOTES

PRIORITIES **SMALL VICTORIES**

NOTES

THOUGHTS AND DOODLES

APPOINTMENTS

PERSON:
DATE:
LOCATION:

PERSON:
DATE:
LOCATION:

PERSON:
DATE:
LOCATION:

PERSON:
DATE:
LOCATION:

PERSON:
DATE:
LOCATION:

PERSON:
DATE:
LOCATION:

PERSON:
DATE:
LOCATION:

I GOT IT DONE

☐ ☐

THIS MONTH

IMPORTANT DATES

THINGS I CAN DO FOR MYSELF THAT WOULD BRING JOY OR HELP ME RECHARGE

PERSON(S) I NEED TO CONNECT WITH

DECISION MAKING

PROJECT: _____

IS IT URGENT?

	YES	NO
IS IT IMPORTANT? YES	STEPS TO DO IT NOW:	PLAN OF ACTION:
NO	DELEGATE TO:	DISCART IT

SELF-CARE CHECKLIST

ACTION	M	T	W	T	F	S	S
	☐	☐	☐	☐	☐	☐	☐
	☐	☐	☐	☐	☐	☐	☐
	☐	☐	☐	☐	☐	☐	☐
	☐	☐	☐	☐	☐	☐	☐
	☐	☐	☐	☐	☐	☐	☐
	☐	☐	☐	☐	☐	☐	☐
	☐	☐	☐	☐	☐	☐	☐
	☐	☐	☐	☐	☐	☐	☐
	☐	☐	☐	☐	☐	☐	☐
	☐	☐	☐	☐	☐	☐	☐

PRODUCTIVITY TRACKER

START	END	TASK	START	END	TASK

PRODUCTIVITY TRACKER

START	END	TASK	START	END	TASK